S0-ACU-788

HEARING

by Robin Nelson

first step nonfiction

Somerset Co. Library
Bridgewater, NJ 08807

Lerner Publications Company · Minneapolis

Hearing is one of my **senses.**

I hear with my ears.

I hear loud **sounds.**
I hear a train.

I hear a jet.

I hear soft sounds.
I hear waves.

I hear a **secret.**

I hear high sounds.
I hear a bird.